METROPOLITAN BOROUGH OF WIRRAL

Please return this book to the Library from which it was borrowed on or before the last date stamped. If not in demand books may be renewed by letter, telephone or in person. Fines will be charged on overdue books at the rate currently determined by the Borough Council.

015150
015683
016954
016179

2 0 DEC 1995

391

MOSS, M.

Traditional costume

S414409

METROPOLITAN BOROUGH OF WIRRAL SCHOOL LIBRARY SERVICE

DEPARTMENT OF LEISURE SERVICES + TOURISM LIBRARIES AND ARTS

Traditional Costume

Miriam Moss

Costumes and Clothes

Accessories
Children's Clothes
Clothes in Cold Weather
Clothes in Hot Weather
Fashionable Clothes
Hair and Make-Up
How Clothes Are Made
Sports Clothes
Theatrical Costume
Traditional Costume
Uniforms
Working Clothes

Some words in this book are printed in **bold**. Their meanings are explained in the glossary on page 30.

METROPOLITAN BOROUGH OF WIRRAL
DEPT. OF LEISURE SERVICES
LIBRARIES AND ARTS DIVISION

SBN ACC.N.	S414409	
LCC. COPY		Y.P.
CLASS No.	391	

First published in 1988 by Wayland (Publishers) Ltd
61 Western Road, Hove, East Sussex BN3 1JD, England.

Consultant: Roger Howarth, the curriculum multi-cultural adviser for East Sussex.

Editor: Deborah Elliott
Designer: Joyce Chester

Cover: Dancers from Bangkok wearing traditional Thai costumes.

© Copyright 1988 Wayland (Publishers) Ltd.

British Library Cataloguing in Publication Data
Moss, Miriam
    Traditional costume.
    1. Folk costume — For children
    I. Title
    391

ISBN 1-85210-101-6

Photosetting by Direct Image Photosetting, Burgess Hill, West Sussex
Printed in Italy by G. Canale & C.S.p.A., Turin
Bound in France by A.G.M.

Contents

Chapter 1	**Traditional Costumes**		4
Chapter 2	**Materials**		6
Chapter 3	**Europe**		
		Northern Europe	8
		Southern Europe	
		Eastern Europe and the USSR	12
Chapter 4	**North and South America**		
		Canada and the USA	14
		Central and South America	16
Chapter 5	**Asia**		
		The Indian sub-continent	18
		The Middle East	20
		The Far East	22
		Southeast Asia	24
Chapter 6	**Africa**		26
Chapter 7	**Australasia**		28
	Glossary		30
	Books to read		30
	Index		31

Chapter 1
Traditional Costumes

There is a rich variety of clothes and costumes worn as traditional dress by people throughout the world. Different regions in most countries have different costumes. This is because, long ago, travelling from one part of a country to another was very difficult, so ideas about dress were rarely exchanged. Special regional styles of dress were usually passed down from one generation to another. Today, in remote parts of the world — in mountainous regions, thick **rainforests** and on some islands — people still dress as their ancestors did centuries ago. In other parts of the world, where travelling is easier, ideas about dress are exchanged so

All over the world, people dress in spectacular, bright costumes for traditional festivals. These dancers are taking part in a carnival in Port of Spain, Trinidad.

quickly that the everyday clothes people wear are very similar.

Most traditional clothes and costumes are only worn on special occasions. They play an important part in ceremonies, festivals and celebrations. They can show someone's rank, religion and, sometimes, even whether they are married or not. The spectacle of the brilliantly-coloured costumes, and the music and dancing, create a great sense of excitement. Some traditional costumes are only worn by people taking part in special activities, like matadors in Spain or the royal Greek guards.

Sometimes clothes are traditional to the people of a whole country, like the kilts worn in Scotland. These costumes are often called 'national costumes' and play an important part in a country's tourist industry. Many people wear 'national' costumes on special occasions, like at the opening ceremony of the Olympics and at ceremonies or functions where they are representing their country.

Above **Royal Greek soldiers in traditional costume guarding the Tomb of the Unknown Soldier, before the Houses of Parliament in Athens.**

Spanish matadors parade in front of the crowd before the bullfight. They are wearing richly decorated suits and colourful capes.

Chapter
2

Materials

At first, regional clothes were only made out of the materials found locally, like trees and plants. Leaves were plaited into clothes, and straw and feathers were also used. The Aztecs, who lived long ago in what is now Mexico,

Below In countries all over the world, traditional costumes are often made from materials found locally. The traditional clothes worn by people living high in the cold Himalayan Mountains are made from warm materials such as wool that are suitable for the climate.

Above Cowboys who do tough and physical jobs wear clothes made from strong, long-lasting materials. Traditionally, they wear hard-wearing, denim jeans, strong, leather boots and belts and cotton shirts.

Flemish people come from Flanders, an area of Europe consisting of parts of France, Belgium and the Netherlands. This woman wears a traditional bonnet made from Flemish lace.

made a material called *ixtle* from the leaves of the cactus plants growing around their homes. They wove the tough, white *ixtle* fibres into a coarse cloth. Today, the Yuracare Indians from the Amazon rainforest in South America make clothes from the bark of trees which they stamp with painted designs. In sheep-rearing areas of the world, traditional costumes are made from wool and sheepskin.

Clothes and costumes developed as protection against the weather, so the kind of traditional costumes worn often depend on the climate of a country. In colder, northern climates the skins of **caribou**, seals and reindeer as well as the feathers from birds are used to make costumes. Other people, living in cold, mountainous regions, protect themselves by weaving the wool and hair from goats and **llama** into warm, woollen clothes. Traditional clothes also developed to fit different lifestyles and types of work. The cowboys of North America herd cattle across kilometres of dry, dusty plains. They wear hard-wearing jeans, leather boots and broad-rimmed hats called stetsons. In some parts of the USA, like Texas, this has become a traditional costume.

Traditional clothes and costumes were made from cotton in regions where cotton was cultivated locally. Similarly, **flax**, which grows in the moist, cool parts of Belgium, Central Europe, Russia and New Zealand, was cultivated to make linen. Other materials such as corduroy, velveteen and **calico** developed after cotton. In the Flemish town of Cambrai, linen was woven into a fine material and called cambric. This was used to make shirts, blouses and lace.

Fustian was first made in a suburb of Cairo, in Egypt, called El Fustat and **gingham** possibly got its name from the Malaysian word *ging-gang*. Hundreds of materials are now used to make costumes and clothes all over the world. Today, many of these are **mass-produced** in factories.

For thousands of years people have used natural dyes to colour their clothes and costumes. These are made from animals (like the red dye from the cochineal beetle), minerals (like iron-rust which makes a reddy-brown colour), and plants (like those made from moss and tree bark). These are still used in parts of the world today, although many dyes are now manufactured in factories. Many other skills are necessary to make the attractive and unusual costumes found all over the world.

Patterned African material and Scottish tartans are made by weaving different coloured threads into checks or stripes. Many traditional costumes are decorated with bright, elaborate **embroidery** and jewellery is crafted from gold, silver, beads, precious and semi-precious stones.

Chapter 3

Europe

Northern Europe

In southern Germany a **bodice**, often beautifully embroidered with silver thread, is traditionally worn by women. It laces up the front over a blouse with large, puffed sleeves. An apron is worn over a long, full skirt. For men, a velvet tunic or long coat over velvet knee breeches is the traditional form of dress. Embroidered, leather shorts and braces called *lederhosen* are also worn in the Alps. Each region has a different style of hat. There are straw hats, ones with ribbons or woollen pompoms and in some regions lovely bridal crowns called *schappel* are worn.

In Holland, skirts are made of striped, woollen material over as many as twenty petticoats. The tightly-fitting blouse has lace embroidery around the neck and the large apron is tied with bright material around the

The members of this German band are wearing a style of traditional *lederhosen* (shorts) that reach to the knees, and braces.

waist. This tradition arose from the **superstition** that aprons would protect the wearer from **werewolves**. Clogs, or *klompen*, are worn on the feet. The head-dress is a pointed, stiff, lace cap with turned-back wings on each side.

A Scotsman's traditional everyday dress is a **tweed** jacket, a kilt, white shirt and long socks with thick, brown **brogue** shoes. He wears a **sporran** made of leather. For highland dancing men wear black doublets (close-fitting jackets) of velvet or cloth. They also have white *jabots* (frills) made of lace at their necks and black, leather belts with a silver buckle. Often a *skean dhu* (dagger) fits down the side of their stockings. A woman's dancing costume is a fine, pleated kilt with a velvet jacket, fastened at the waist over a white, lace-fronted blouse. Both men and women wear black dancing pumps.

Above These beautifully decorated Dutch clogs were handcarved by the groom for his bride as a wedding present.

Below A traditional English costume worn by Morris dancers. White trousers and a shirt are worn with bells around the legs.

Southern Europe

In France each province has its own traditional costume. Some are still worn on Sundays. In Brittany, in the north-west of France, men wear knee-length, baggy, white, linen trousers called *bragon bas*. They wear embroidered waistcoats with silver buttons, and wooden *sabots* (clogs) on their feet. Women wear full-skirted, embroidered dresses with tight bodices. Their *coifs* (hats) are made of lace — sometimes as much as 45 cm high! The traditional headgear for men is a wide-brimmed hat.

Italian women, who live in the country, traditionally wear aprons and full dresses decorated with elaborate embroidery and strips of coloured material. Men wear brightly-coloured, linen shirts and waistcoats. Their knee-breeches can be tight or baggy and are held up by a belt which, in Campagna, can be as much as 15 cm wide! In the south women

Above Dancing dresses are usually made of many metres of material so they will swirl and follow the movement of the dance. The dress worn by this Spanish dancer is made from metres of beautiful, white lace.

Left An outstanding feature of the traditional costume worn by women in Brittany, France is the *coif* which is a lace hat. You can see from the photograph just how tall and eye-catching the *coif* can be.

wear bright scarves. In some places a kind of bonnet is worn made from stiffened, gold, lace thread. In Lombardy, women put their hair up in buns which they stud with a **halo** of bright, silver pins.

Women from Andalusia in Spain, where **flamenco** music and dancing developed, wear a long or a short, flounced dress with full, elbow-length sleeves and a tight-fitting bodice down to the hips. The full skirt has several layers of frills and is worn with a starched, white, cotton, petticoat. The famous head-dress is a fine, lace shawl called a *mantilla*

These girls from the South Tirol in Italy are wearing costumes that are traditional to their region. Notice their black, fingerless gloves. Also notice the embroidered bands on the front of their skirts.

worn over a carved comb. Men wear very tight-fitting trousers cut above the waist with a *chaleco* (short jacket) and waistcoat. Both men and women wear strong dancing shoes to stand up to the quick drumming footbeats of the dance.

Eastern Europe and the USSR

There are thousands of regional costumes found in the USSR. In the Ukraine, women's full skirts are often embroidered with geometric patterns. Over the blouse and skirt a *sarafan* (sleeveless bodice) is worn, with petticoats underneath. The floral head-dresses have long ribbons hanging down the back. Both men and women wear red boots. The men tuck very full red, white or blue trousers into their boots. They also wear an embroidered, white, linen shirt, a colourful, wide sash and a fur cap of grey or white **astrakhan**. The many different traditional costumes worn in Siberia, in the cold north of the country, are based on Mongolian styles. The costumes are made of fur, skin and felt and decorated with simple patterns. Men and women wear similar clothes except that the women's costume is ankle-length and the men's tunic is shorter.

The basic traditional costume worn by these Polish boys and girls is similar but how many different colours can you pick out?

The matching bright red boots and shoes and embroidered costumes traditionally worn by the 'Morianas', a dance troupe from the USSR, show they all belong to the same group.

In Poland the area around Lowicz is famous for its striped, woollen material. The most popular costume is perhaps the one from Krakow which is bright and ornate. Both men and women in Poland wear sheepskin coats with the wool worn on the inside. The outside is decorated with beautiful stitching, or leather strips are sewn on.

The Hungarian costume is among the most attractive in Europe. Bright, full skirts with layers of petticoats are worn by women while men wear full, flared, white trousers which look like **culottes**.

In Yugoslavia many of the traditional costumes have coins hanging from chains around the neck or fixed on to aprons. These coins are the woman's **dowry**, given to her future husband on their marriage.

Chapter 4
North and South America

Canada and the USA

The Indians, or Native Americans, were the original inhabitants of Canada and the USA, although many other people from all over the world have now settled there, bringing with them the costumes from their original countries. The Canadian Indian costume is a wrap-around skirt, an apron or a type of loin cloth called a *breechclout*, leggings, shirts and cloaks made from buffalo skins. Buckskin **moccasins** and fur mittens are also worn. The Native Americans who settled in the

At the fair held to mark the two hundredth anniversary of Medford Village, New Jersey, people dressed in costumes worn by the first Europeans who settled in the USA.

USA wore the same basic costume as the Canadian Indians. Some, however, wore a special shirt made from buckskin and decorated with tufts of horsehair, human hair, animal skins, braid or beadwork. The decoration of the costume identified the area of each tribe. Indians believed in the **supernatural** power of animal skins, feathers and claws, thinking that the strength of the animal would be passed on to the wearer. The famous eagle feather head-dresses were first worn by the Plains tribes. A single eagle's feather was awarded for each brave deed. The Iroquois Indian head-dress is a tight-fitting cap of skin or feathers. Another group of Woodland Indians, the Huron, wear a head-dress called 'the roach', shaped like a crest and made from dyed horsehair.

The traditional **Inuit** costume from further north has changed very little over the years. A thick, warm, long-sleeved jacket, called a *parka*, is worn which is made from caribou skin. Both men and women wear sealskin boots, called *kamiks*.

Above **Canadian Indian dancers in Banff National Park, Canada wearing the traditional costumes of their ancestors. Notice the fur, feathers and beads in their costumes.**

Traditional *parkas* worn by Alaskans are both attractive and extremely practical as the temperature in Alaska can fall as low as −12°C. The *parkas* are made out of a thick cloth or duffle material and decorated with embroidery in floral or geometric designs.

Central and South America

The different Mexican traditional costumes developed depending on whether they were being worn for work, fiestas, religious processions or dancing. Today, in more isolated areas, women still spin their costumes and clothes from cotton thread or **henequen** fibre. Many of their designs and embroidery of birds, animals and flowers come from ancient Aztec and Mayan symbols. The women's basic costume is a *huipil* which is a kind of tunic dress made from wool or cotton and a head-dress called a *quechquemitl*. This is a triangular **poncho** which covers the upper part of the body. The skirts are full and are

Above People all over the world probably wear a costume that is traditional to their home country at national celebrations. This Mexican boy wears a form of traditional dress to a Mexican festival in Santa Barbara, USA.

Left Bolivians traditionally wear clothes made from llama and alpaca wool. They are hard-wearing and designed to be warm, practical and attractively patterned.

worn with several petticoats.

Bolivians wear their most colourful and elaborate costumes at carnivals. The clothes are made out of cotton or a coarse, hard-wearing, woollen cloth made from **alpaca** and llama wool. Women wear bright skirts called *polleras* with lots of petticoats underneath.

A brightly-coloured, long-sleeved blouse is worn with a colourful, fringed, woollen cape or shawl. Bolivian babies are carried in a knotted blanket which is worn over the shawl.

Women often wear a bowler or derby hat made of felt which is soaked, pounded and then starched or moulded into shape. Bolivian men wear dark trousers and a sash or belt. In summer they wear a sleeveless waistcoat over a shirt. A brightly-woven poncho is worn on top in cold weather. A tight-fitting cap with long ear flaps called a *llucho* or *chullo* is worn in high mountainous regions. This is knitted or woven and can be patterned with symbols of llamas or the sun.

These Peruvians are dressed in traditional costumes as part of a festival at Mauka Llaqta. Their clothes are very brightly coloured and decorated with lots of ribbons.

Chapter 5

Asia

The Indian sub-continent

In India traditional clothes are strongly influenced by religion. The most popular traditional dress for women is the *sari* which can be made from cotton, nylon, silk or muslin. It is a length of material that is wrapped around a petticoat, pleated at the front and tucked into the top. It is worn over a tight-fitting bodice called a *choli*. The long end of the *sari*, the *pallu*, is draped over the left shoulder and worn over the head or tucked into the waist. The border of the *sari* is usually patterned, often with elephants, trees, **mangoes** and buffalo.

In the north, the people of Kashmir weave *saris* in famous patterns from which the Scottish paisley pattern originated. Hand-printed muslin *saris* are made in Sangammer and beautiful silk *saris* with borders of silver and gold **brocade** are made in Varanasi in

The dancers performing at this wedding ceremony in India wear special costumes decorated with metallic threads.

Left Dancers traditionally wear two or three eye-catching colours to identify themselves as part of a group and to create a special effect.

Uttar Pradesh. In Kashmir and the Punjab and in parts of Pakistan, many Muslim women wear a knee-length tunic called a *kameez* over trousers that are gathered at the ankles, called *salwar*.

In India, a *dhoti*, which is a length of silk or cotton material tied or wrapped around the lower part of the body in different ways, is the traditional male costume. Either a shirt or a loose tunic is worn wrapped around the shoulders and chest. Sikhs wear *churidar* which are tight, white trousers with buttoned, knee-length jackets. Punjabi Sikh men wear white shirts and a coloured *dhoti* under a black waistcoat and an elaborate turban.

This mother from Pakistan has taken a lot of time and trouble to make and decorate her child's costume. Notice the decoration on his hat.

The Middle East

In Saudi Arabia, Muslim women wear loose-fitting, ankle-length dresses made from silk or cotton. A large, loose, black cloak is worn over the dress and covers the head and face.

For special occasions men wear a *gumbaz* (a wide-sleeved coat). On top of this is worn a large, sleeveless cloak called an *abayeh* made from wool or cotton. It is woven in stripes and is often embroidered around the neck and down the front edges. A *keffiyeh* which is a head veil or scarf, is worn over a white skull cap. Head ropes, called *agal*, sometimes made of metal threads, keep the scarf in place.

The traditional costumes of the nomadic Bedouin, who live in many countries in the north of Africa and the Middle East, are brighter. The embroidery on the women's costumes, the head-dresses and hair styles, the jewellery and the pattern and colour of the bright, cotton materials show where the wearer comes from.

Above This woman from Qatar wears an eye-catching dress and a traditional veil to cover her face.

In Egypt the traditional costume worn by women is a simple dress that has a neckline decorated with embroidery, beads, pearls or braid. At festivals ornate necklaces, bracelets and anklets are popular. Full trousers are worn under the dress and a long veil is attached to a headband, sometimes covered with gold coins. Men wear white shirts and loose, white trousers underneath a *galabia* which is a long-sleeved, cotton garment. A white turban, red **fez** or a tight-fitting skull cap are popular forms of head-dress.

Bedouin guards from Dubai wear white, cotton robes that reflect the intense heat and keep them cool.

These women from Bahrain are wearing special costumes decorated with gold thread to celebrate the Muslim festival of *Id-ul-Fitr*.

The Far East

The Japanese traditional costume is the *kimono*. This is a loose robe wrapped over in front and tied at the waist with a sash called an *obi*. The *obi* is usually tied at the back, though it is tied at the front for funerals and worn with a black *kimono* decorated with family **crests**. *Kimonos* are made of brocade, silk or cotton, dyed in rich colours.

In southern China the traditional costume is based on loose trousers and long-sleeved jackets worn by both men and women. In some provinces calf-length trousers, a short, black skirt with a coloured jacket, a striped apron and tight **gaiters** up to the knees are worn. In one particular province women wear pointed black hats and fasten silver plaques down the front of their jackets. The Chinese embroider mysterious dragons, waves, lucky symbols and clouds on to their traditional, highly ornamental costumes.

The traditional costumes of Mongolia, to the north of China, are designed for riding. Men and women wear a similar costume made of wool. The coats, called *dels*, are often dark blue or red, with a bright green sash tied around the waist. The hem and neck are braided and the trousers and decoration are in contrasting colours to the coat. Men wear hats made of sheepskin, wool, astrakhan or felt, decorated with coloured beads.

Left The Japanese girl on the right is dressed in a traditional silk *kimono* for a party. The bright red sash tied around her waist is called an *obi*.

Opposite A young girl dressed up in a beautiful costume for the *Cheung Chau* festival in Hong Kong. Notice how face make-up adds to the overall effect of her costume.

Southeast Asia

Thailand is famous for its silk which comes in brilliant peacock colours like turquoise, scarlet, gold and flame. Thai women wear a wrap-around *sarong* skirt with a fitted, long-sleeved jacket. In the Philippine Islands Catholic women wear long dresses made of brightly patterned silk for special occasions; some are styled with a round 'boat neck' and with wide, puffed sleeves. The dresses can be very full with long trains hanging down the back.

In Indonesia the most popular form of traditional dress is the *kain*, which is a long, wrap-around skirt. Cotton is the most widely used material and is delicately dyed in **batik** designs. Sometimes the *kain* is beautifully woven with metal threads. Over the *kain*, women wear a long-sleeved jacket called a *kebaya*. Men from the island of Sumatra traditionally wear a *kain* with a white shirt or with baggy trousers. In Malaysia many people wear clothes made of *kain songet* — cloth embroidered with gold thread.

You can imagine how much work has gone into making these traditional Thai costumes. They have been decorated with intricate embroidery and beadwork.

Above At this Islamic school in Kuala Lumpur, Malaysia the pupils wear traditional clothes as part of their uniform. The girls wear *mini telekong* (head-dresses), *baju kurong* (loose blouses) and *sarung* (loose, ankle-length skirts).

Left Traditional wedding costumes worn by Malay brides and grooms throughout Malaysia are made of *kain songet*. This is a special material, usually in one single colour, that is embroidered with gold thread.

Chapter 6

Africa

In Ethiopia the traditional costume for both men and women is a long, white cotton dress with long sleeves. Over this they wear a *shamma* which is a long length of material made of white muslin, cotton or calico. The *shamma* can have a border woven in bright geometric designs. It is worn draped around the body in different ways depending on age, importance and region or in special ways when attending church, at celebrations or when visiting someone important. Sometimes men wear long, white trousers and tunics which, on feast days, are replaced by ones made of striped silk. High, white, round turbans are traditionally worn by many Ethiopian men while others plait their hair elaborately and form it into special shapes.

In Ghana, in West Africa, women's costumes are made up of brightly-printed cotton drapery which they decorate with heavy necklaces and bracelets of beads and gold. In northern Nigeria it is traditional for high-ranking Hausa

Mapoch women from South Africa display their traditional costumes decorated with elaborate beadwork and colourful designs. Notice their heavy ornamental jewellery.

A colourful traditional costume of Sierra Leone. The cotton material is cool and comfortable to wear.

This brightly coloured costume is traditionally worn by some women who live in the Upper Volta.

men to wear loose, flowing, ankle-length gowns which are beautifully embroidered with symbolic patterns. Underneath the gowns, baggy trousers are worn, made up from metres of material and gathered at the ankles. Nigerian women wear cool, wide-sleeved tunics in brilliantly-printed fabrics which are cleverly arranged in many different styles with matching head-dresses.

The Zulu people of South Africa use leopard and lion skins in their traditional dress. Others decorate their bodies with dyes and tattoos.

The height and elaborate design of this Zulu head-dress can be a sign of the wearer's importance.

Chapter 7

Australasia

The traditional costume of the Maoris from New Zealand is only worn by folk groups and at special celebrations. It is made using flax fibre woven by hand. Maori finger weaving is called *taniko*. The patterns made from the fibres dyed black, yellow or reddish-brown, have special names and meanings — a downward zig-zag represents the waves of the

The traditional costumes of New Zealand Maoris are often made from flax which is grown locally. These Maori dancers are wearing skirts made from flax.

sea, for example. Women traditionally wear a *pari* which is a bodice made in a *taniko* design. The *piupiu* skirt is made from tight rolls of flax and is worn by both men and women. High-ranking Maoris wear beautiful cloaks made of white, green, bluish-black and red feathers.

Australia is a country made up of many different cultures. The Aborigines, the original inhabitants of Australia, paint their bodies, using substances such as chalk, for special festivals and celebrations.

As many Australians originally came from countries like Vietnam, Turkey, Germany and Britain, many wear the traditional costume of these countries on special occasions. It is common, for example, to see boys and girls of Greek origin wearing Greek costume at a traditional Australian festival.

Above Australian cattle hands wearing hats, jeans and cotton shirts. This style of dress is traditional to areas of the outback where people work with cattle and sheep.

Right Many Australians are of European and Asian origin. It is quite common to see people dressed in the costumes of many different countries at Australian festivals. These girls are dressed in Polish costume at a carnival in Parramatta Park, New South Wales.

Glossary

Alpaca A South American mammal related to the llama, with dark, shaggy hair.
Astrakhan A fur, usually black or grey, made from the closely curled wool from sheep found in Astrakhan in the USSR.
Batik A way of printing fabric where the parts not dyed are covered in wax.
Bodice The upper part of a woman's dress or a tight-fitting garment, sometimes worn laced over a blouse.
Brocade A fabric woven with a raised design, often using gold or silver thread.
Brogue A sturdy walking shoe.
Calico A type of cotton cloth.
Caribou A large North American reindeer.
Crest A symbol of a family such as a badge.
Culottes Flared, knee-length or ankle-length trousers cut to look like a skirt.
Dowry The property given by a woman to her husband on marriage.
Embroidery A pattern sewn on to fabric.
Fez A brimless hat.
Flamenco A type of dance performed to guitar music.
Flax A plant whose fibres are woven into linen.
Fustian A hard-wearing fabric of cotton mixed with flax or wool.
Gaiters Coverings for the legs which come to below the knee.
Gingham A cotton cloth with stripes or checks.
Halo A ring of light painted or drawn round the heads of holy people in pictures.
Henequen A plant that grows in Mexico. The fibre is used to make rope and coarse fabric.
Inuit People from Arctic North America and Greenland.
Llama A South American animal belonging to the camel family but without any humps.
Mangoes The oval fruit of the mango tree which has a smooth rind and a sweet, juicy flesh.
Mass-produce To make a large number of goods using machinery.
Moccasins A soft, leather shoe without a heel originally worn by North American Indians.
Poncho A cloak, originally from South America, made from a triangular or circular piece of cloth, with a hole in the middle for the head.
Rainforest Dense forest found in tropical areas of heavy rainfall.
Sarong A skirt-like garment worn wrapped around the body by both men and women in Malaya and the Pacific Islands.
Sporran A large pouch, sometimes made of fur, worn hanging from a belt in front of a kilt in Scottish Highland dress. Originally it was used to protect the body but is now often used as a purse.
Supernatural Something that is spiritual and not of this world.
Superstition A misguided belief in magic.
Tweed A rough, woollen cloth.
Werewolves People in folk stories who have been changed into wolves by being bewitched.

Books to read

If you would like to find out more about traditional costume, you might like to read the following books:
Clothes (Macdonald Educational, 1977)
Clothes in Cold Weather by Miriam Moss [Wayland (Publishers Ltd), 1988]
Clothes in Hot Weather by Miriam Moss [Wayland (Publishers Ltd), 1988]
Costumes and Clothes by Jean Cooke [Wayland (Publishers Ltd), 1986]
Exploring Clothes by Brenda Ralph Lewis [Wayland (Publishers Ltd), 1988]
Folk Costumes of the World by Robert Harrold (Blandford Press, 1978)
Just Look at Clothes by Brenda Ralph Lewis (Macdonald Educational, 1985)
Living Here series [Wayland (Publishers Ltd),]
National Costume [BPC Publishing Ltd, 1970]
The Anatomy of Costume by Robert Selbie [Bell & Hyman Ltd, 1982]
World Costumes by Angela Bradshaw [A & C Black Ltd, 1977]

Index

Aborigines 29
African costumes 26-7
Alaskan costumes **15**
Animal skins 12, 15
    buffalo 14
    caribou 7, 15
    leopard 27
    lion 27
    reindeer 7
    seals 7, 15
    sheep 7, 13, 23
Aprons
    Canadian Indian 14
    Chinese 22
    Dutch 8, 9
    German 8
    Italian 10
    Yugoslavian 13
Asian costumes 18-25
Australian costumes 28-9

Bedouin costumes 20
Belgian costumes 7
Belts 10, 17
    leather 9
Blouses 7
    Bolivian 17
    Dutch 8
    German 8
    Scottish 9
Bodice 11
    choli 18
    pari 29
    sarafan 12
Bolivian costumes 17
Boots
    cowboy 7
    kamiks 15
    leather 7
    red 11
Breeches
    German 8
    Italian 10
British costumes 5, 9

Canadian Indians 14, 15

Caps
    chullo 17
    Dutch 19
    fur 12
    lace 9
    skull 20
Capes
    matadors **5**
    woollen 17
Central American costumes 16
Chinese costumes 22
Clogs
    Dutch 9
    French 10
Coats
    dels 22
    German 8
    gumbaz 20
    Mongolian 23
    sheepskin 13
Costumes
    dancing **4**, 5, 9, **10**, 11, 16, **19**
    for special occasions 5, 16-7, 26, 29
    religious 5, 18
    woollen 7
Cowboys **6**, 7

Decorations
    batik 24
    beads 7, 15, 20, 23, **24**, **26**
    body 27, 29
    braid 15, 20
    brocade 18
    embroidery 7, 8, 10, 12, 20, 22, 27
    geometric 26
    gold 7, 18
    jewellery 7, 20, **26**
    pearls 20
    silver 7
    symbols 15, 16, 22, **23**, 27
Dresses
    Egyptian 20
    embroidered 10
    Ethiopian 26

flamenco 11
Italian 10
Philippine 24
Saudi Arabian 20

Egypt 7, 20
Ethiopia 26
European costumes
    Dutch 8-9
    French 10
    German 8
    Hungary 13
    Italian 10-11
    Poland 13, **29**
    Scottish 9
    Spanish **5**, 11
    USSR 12
    Yugoslavia

Far Eastern costumes 22-3
Flamenco music 11

Gaiters 22
German costumes 8
Ghana 26
Gowns 27
Greek costumes 5, 29

Hats
    bowler 17
    broad-rimmed 7
    coifs 10
    derby 17
    German 8
    pointed 22
    schappel 8
    stetsons 7
    straw 8
Hair styles
    Bedouin 20
    Ethiopian 26
Head-dresses
    Bedouin 20
    Brittany 10
    Dutch 9
    eagle feather 15

fez 20
Mexican 16
Nigerian 27
Spanish 11
turban 19, 20, 26
USSR 12
Zulu **27**

Jackets
   Chinese 22
   kebaya 24
   parka 15
   Sikh 19
   tweed 9
   velvet 9
Japanese costumes 22, **23**
Jeans 7, **29**
Jewellery 7, 20, 26

Kilts 5, 9
Kimonos 22

Lace 7, 9, 11
Lederhosen 8

Malaysian costumes 7, **25**
Maoris 28
Materials
   astrakhan 12, 13
   brocade 18, 22
   calico 7, 26
   cambric 7
   corduroy 7
   cotton 7, 16, 17, 19, 20, 22, 26

feathers 6, 7, 15, 29
felt 12, 17, 23
flax 7, 28, 29
gingham 7
hair 7, 15
ixtle 7
leather 9, 13
linen 7, 10
muslin 26
plants 6, 7
silk 18, 19, 20, 22, 24, 26
straw 6
trees 6, 7
wool 7, 8, 12, 13, 16, 17, 20, 23
Mexican costumes 6-7, 16-17
Middle Eastern costumes 20-21
Morris dancers **9**

New Zealand 7, 28-9
Nigeria 26, 27
North American costumes
   Canadian Indian 14
   cowboys 7
   Native Americans 14, 15

Pakistani costumes 19
Petticoats
   Bolivian 17
   Dutch 8
   Hungarian 13
   Mexican 17
   Spanish 11
   USSR 12
Ponchos 16, 17

Saudi Arabian costumes 20
Scarves 11
   keffiyeh 20
Scottish costumes 5
Shawls 17
Shirts 7, 17, 19, 20, 22, 24
   buckskin 15
   buffalo skin 14
   embroidered 12
   linen 10
Shoes
   brogues 9
   dancing 9, 11
   moccasins 14
   pumps 9
Sikh costumes 19
Skirts 8, 11, 12, 14, 16, 17, 29
South American costumes **16**, 17
Southeast Asian costumes 24-5
Spanish costumes 5, **10**

Thailand 24
Trousers
   Bolivian 17
   Brittany 10
   Chinese 22
   culottes 13
   Egyptian 20
   Ethiopian 26
   Hausa 27
   Hungarian 13
   Inuit 15
   Italian 11
   linen 10

Acknowledgements

The Publisher would like to thank the following for providing the pictures for this book: David Bowden 29 (bottom); Bruce Coleman 9 (bottom), 11, 13, 14, 15, 16 (bottom), 23, 24, 27 (bottom); Hutchison Library 5 (bottom), 9 (top), 20 (top); Miriam Moss 6 (left); Christine Osborne 20 (bottom), 21, 25 (top), 29 (top); Axel Poignant 28; Save the Children 17 (Caroline Penn), 19 (bottom, Jill Brown); Topham Picture Library 26, 27 (top); Wayland Picture Library 5 (top), 18, 25 (bottom); ZEFA 4, 6 (right), 7, 8, 10, 12, 16 (top), 19 (top), 22.